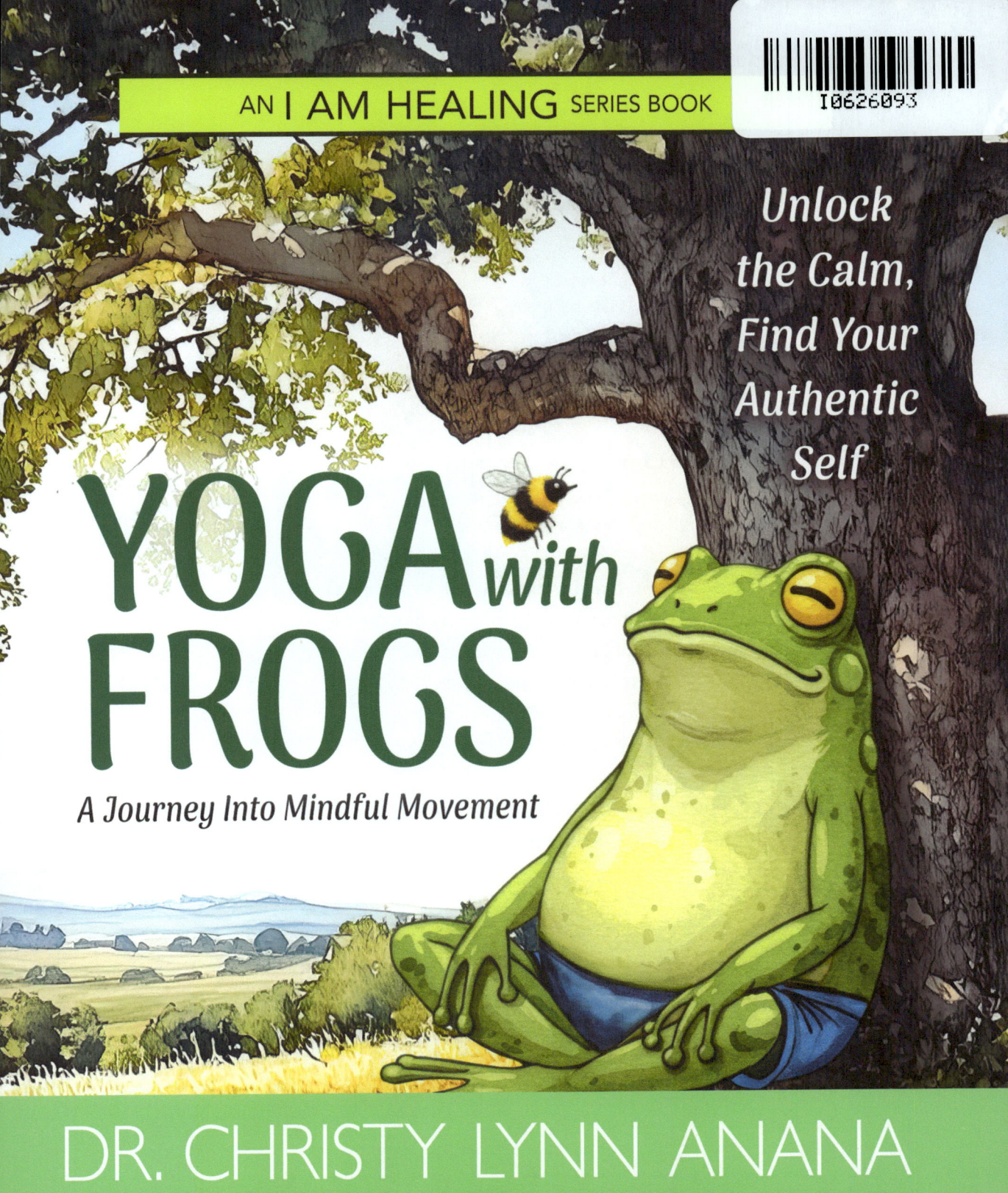

AN **I AM HEALING** SERIES BOOK

Unlock the Calm, Find Your Authentic Self

YOGA with FROGS

A Journey Into Mindful Movement

DR. CHRISTY LYNN ANANA

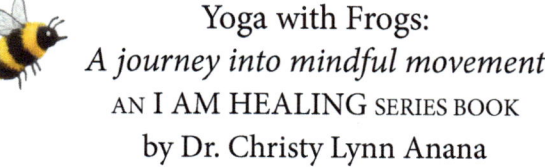

Yoga with Frogs:
A journey into mindful movement
AN I AM HEALING SERIES BOOK
by Dr. Christy Lynn Anana

Anana Press
ISBN: 978-1-957400-20-4
Book illustrations by Suzanne Parrott
Cover and Interior design/layout by Suzanne Parrott

ChristyLynnAnana.com

Printed in the
United States of America

Notice how you
feel right now.

Today is a good day
to go on a journey into
mindful movement.

Breathe

into each new pose.

Find your strong mountain pose
with your feet activated to feel the ground.

Move your hands together
at your heart. You feel
your heart beating. You feel
yourself breathing.

Relax.

Notice what feelings
bubble up.

Allow the feelings to pour
from your heart.

If you want, gently close
your eyes and see yourself
in a place that you feel safe.

With all of those feelings at your heart, gently open your eyes and lift your hands above your head for Upward Mountain pose.

Bring your right foot back into a lunge
while bending your left knee.
When you feel strong,
bring your arms up for Warrior I.

Breathe.

Whisper to yourself,
"I am strong,"
and then bring your arms straight
across for Warrior 2.

Bring your feet together. Do the
same for your other side. Bring your
left foot back into a lunge while
bending your left knee.

When you feel strong, bring your arms up for Warrior 1.

Then arms straight across back to Warrior 2.

Breathe.

Place your feet back together. Bend your knees while lifting your arms for Chair Position.

Straighten legs
and return to
Upward Mountain
and then Mountain.

Breathe.

Now, look like a Star.

See yourself as part of a galaxy of stars

Breathe.

Bend your knees and float your arms
back and forth for Sunflower Pose

Allow anything you don't need to be released
from your body. Make room for happy thoughts.

Breathe.

Side angle and other side angle.

Gently with your body, return to
your strong Mountain pose.

Breathe in, return to
upward Mountain.

Relax.

Again and Again

Poses: Top (l-r) : Mountain, Upward Mountain, Tree;
Bottom (l-r): Chair, Star, Sunflower

Poses: Top (l-r) : Side Angle, Downward Dog;   Middle: Warrior 2;
Bottom (l-r): Bridge, Warrior 2

Sit in your chair with your feet flat.

Twist to one side and then the other.

Rest your head by cradling it on your arms.

Relax.

If you feel comfortable, you can choose to close your eyes. Imagine that you are sitting with a strong tree up against your back or resting in a peaceful meadow.

Relax.

Breathe.

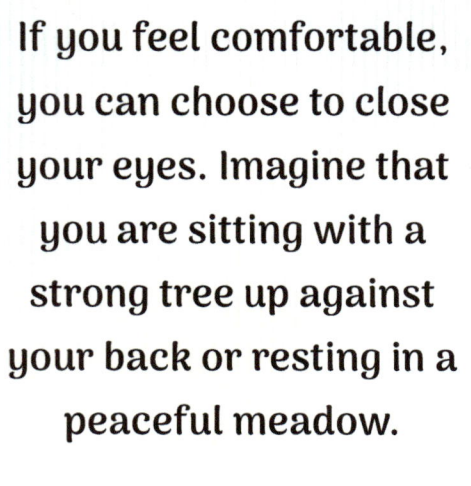

You feel like you can take a real rest. Just like the tree, you can get what you need from the earth as you feel your feet on the ground. The sunshine feeds you with light. You can bend with the wind.

Relax.

Inhale Slowly.

Stay here as long
as you need.

Very gently coming back.
Wiggle your fingers and
toes. Lift up your head.
Open your eyes, and
give yourself a stretch.
Feeling all the good
feelings that come from
mindful movement and
relaxation. Do this as
often as you can so you
can feel better.

Breathe.

Yoga with Frogs is well-suited for classrooms with students of all ages. You can practice at your desk or table. Doing yoga alongside children helps everyone de-stress. Collectively, we can get rid of anxiety and soar high.

We have a path to connect to who we truly are, and we engage the strong voice inside who guides us to help us achieve our highest goals.

I wish you well!

www.ingramcontent.com/pod-product-compliance
Lightning Source LLC
Chambersburg PA
CBHW041445120626
46547CB00002B/359